Wri
Pock

CW00402245

OCR Gateway A
Physics 1, 2, 3 and 4

For GCSE Physics
Higher Tier

For those students who don't find physics the easiest of the sciences...hopefully this will help.

How to use this pocket booster

Each topic has a QR code at the end of the page. If you download a free QR code reader on your phone, this will then take you to the video about that topic on YouTube.

If you see a formula in a box – You need to learn it for the exam.

The key idea of this book is to carry it with you and just take those few minutes to read a couple of pages to check you know it. Learn it, revisit it and then review it again. The more you do this, the more information you will retain.

I hope that you find this book useful.

Subscribe to Wright Science on YouTube to for a full set of videos to support you in your GCSE science studies.

ISBN-13: 9781093231977

2019

P1
Matter

P1.1: The Model of the Atom

Over the years, the theory of the atom has changed. There are four key scientists you need to know about:

Democritus and Leucippus

Thought that eventually you reach a point where things cannot be cut up any more and this would be an atom. They said atoms are too small to see.

John Dalton

Carried out experiments to see how elements combine. His model of the atom was a very small indestructible sphere.

He thought all atoms in an element are the same but the atoms in one element are different from atoms in other elements.

J.J. Thomson

Investigated cathode rays which were given out by hot metals.

He discovered cathode rays are made from negative particles called electrons.

He suggested the plum-pudding model to explain the neutral atom.

Ernest Rutherford (With Geiger and Marsden)

Discovered some materials emit positively charged alpha particles. He fired these alpha particles at thin sheets of gold foil.

If the plum-pudding model had been correct, the alpha particles would have passed straight through but he found some alpha particles were deflected.

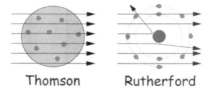

Thomson   Rutherford

To explain this, he suggested an atom is made of a tiny, positively charged nucleus with electrons around the outside. The electrons were orbiting around the nucleus like the planets in our Solar System.

Niels Bohr

Bohr suggested that electrons can only move in fixed orbits called electron shells.

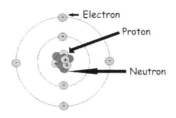

Size of the Atom

An atom is about 1×10^{-10}m in diameter. The radius of the nucleus is 1×10^{-15}m

P1.2.1: Density and PAG P1

Density tells you how much mass there is in a certain volume.

Density (kg/m³) = Mass (kg) ÷ Volume (m³)

To measure density, you will need:

- Electronic balance to measure the mass

- Ruler to work out the volume if the object has a regular shape (L × W × D)

- Eureka can and measuring cylinder to work out the volume if the object has an irregular shape.

The density of a material will be altered with a change in the state of matter. This can be explained using particle theory.

In a solid there are more particles in any given volume than in the gas. The more particles, the greater the mass so the density increases.

Density depends upon the arrangement of the particles AND the mass of the particles.

Law of Conservation of Mass: Particles are neither created nor destroyed. If you have 1kg of ice, you will have 1kg of steam when it evaporates (assuming no gas is lost).

P1.2.2: Energy and Temperature

Temperature:
- How hot or cold something is.
- It is measured with a thermometer or temperature sensor.
- Units are $^{\circ}$C or kelvin (K).
- Tells you about the average kinetic energy of the particles.

Energy in a thermal store:
- Measured in joules (J).
- Depends on the arrangement of the particles and how fast they are moving.

When an object is heated it can:
- Change the energy stored in the system to increase the temperature.
- Produce a change of state
- Make chemical reactions happen

When thinking about how materials change, there are two types of change:

A physical change is a change of state. e.g. solid to liquid or dissolving. New substances are not made and it is usually reversible.

A chemical change involves a chemical reaction. A new substance is made. It is usually irreversible.

P1.2.3: Specific Heat Capacity and PAG P5

Specific Heat Capacity: The amount of energy needed to raise the temperature of 1kg of a material by 1K.
Units: J/kg K

The amount of energy needed to raise the temperature of an object depends upon:
- Type of material
- Mass of material
- Temperature rise

When an object is heated, the internal energy is increased. The internal energy relates to the motion, vibration, rotation and arrangement of the particles.

Change in Thermal Energy (J) = Mass (kg) × Specific Heat Capacity (J/kg K) × Change in Temperature (°C)

14

An object with a high specific heat capacity is resistant to changes in temperature. E.g. Water in central heating systems.

An object with a low specific heat capacity will heat up quickly e.g. metal in saucepans

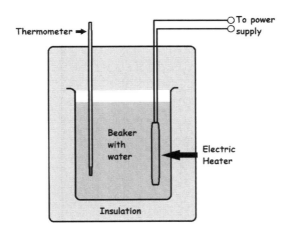

When investigating the energy transferred when heating a substance, you will need to measure:
- Potential difference across the heater
- Current through the heater
- Time the heater is on for

Energy Transferred (J) =
P.d. (V) × Current (A) × Time (s)

To measure the specific heat capacity, you need to use an electronic balance to record the mass of the material being heated.

You need to record the current using an ammeter, the potential difference using a voltmeter and the time using a stop watch.

You use a thermometer to record the temperature rise.

You should repeat the experiment and take the mean, ignoring outliers.

Then calculate the specific heat capacity using the formula from the Physics Formula Sheet in the exam.

If you are asked for sources of potential error, look at the method and diagram they give you and check for:
- Heater not fuller immersed – Some heat is transferred to the surroundings instead of the material.
- Insulation used all around – Any missing insulation means heat will be transferred to the surroundings.
- Location of the thermometer – If it is against the heater, then it is not giving an accurate temperature reading of the whole material.

P1.2.4: Specific Latent Heat

Make sure you remember the processes that lead to the changes of state:

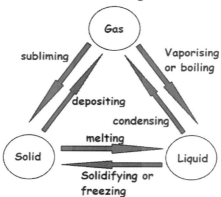

If we plot a graph of how temperature of a substance changes over time when heated, we get a distinctive shape. The plateaus (horizontal bits) are where the internal energy is increasing but is being used to break the intermolecular forces between molecules, so the temperature remains the same.

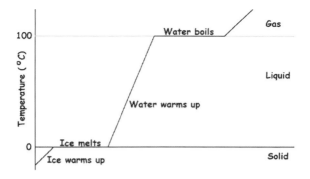

On the diagonal parts, the energy being supplied is increasing the temperature of the substance.

If you are asked to calculate the energy transferred when a substance changes state, you are going to use the specific latent heat formula from the Physics Formula Sheet:

Thermal Energy (J) = Mass (kg) × Specific Latent Heat (J/kg)

There are two specific latent heat terms you need to know:

Specific Latent Heat of Fusion: Energy transferred when 1kg of a substance changes from the solid state to the liquid state, or vice versa.

Specific Latent Heat of Vaporisation: Energy transferred when 1kg of a substance changes from the liquid state to the gas state, or vice versa.

This means you can select the right value from the table of data they provide in the exam question.

Check Your Understanding

1. Explain how ideas about the structure of the atom have changed over time.

2. Name the four scientists who were key to the structure of the atom changing and state their contributions.

3. Explain the difference between temperature and energy in a thermal store.

4. Explain the difference between a physical change and a chemical change.

5. Define the term specific heat capacity.

6. Describe how to work out the specific heat capacity of a material.

7. Define the term specific latent heat of fusion.

P1.3.1: Gas Pressure and Temperature

Gas pressure can best be thought of in an example:

As you blow up a balloon, the number of air particles inside increases. The particles collide with the surface of the balloon and each collision creates a small force. These collisions produce gas pressure. The force that acts on the balloon makes it expand so the balloon gets bigger.

If you add air particles to a container that cannot expand the pressure increases.

When the temperature of a gas increases, the particles gain kinetic energy and therefore collide more frequently with the sides of the container. This leads to an increase in pressure.

To measure the pressure of air inside a container you can use a pressure gauge.

Gas pressure is measured in pascals (Pa).

$$1Pa = 1N/m^2$$
$$1kPa = 1000Pa$$

As the temperature decreases, so does the pressure. If we cooled a gas to absolute zero (0K) then it would have 0Pa of pressure. This can be worked out by extrapolating a graph of results we have collected.·

P1.3.2: Pressure and Volume

Pressure and volume are inversely proportional. This means that if the volume doubles, the pressure will halve.

Exam hint: Be specific in questions asking about patterns. Don't just say increase/decrease. Use words like doubles.

The collisions of the gas particles produce a force at **right angles to the surface**. If the volume is halved, then there will be twice the number of collisions each second with the container.

In the exam you need to be able to use the following formula:
Pressure (Pa) x Volume (m^3) = Constant

This is given to you on the Physics Formula Sheet.

The internal energy of a gas can be increased by:
- Doing work on it
- Heating it

As you do work on a gas, it gets hotter. This leads to the kinetic energy of the particles increasing and so the pressure increases as the particles collide more frequently with the container.

P1.3.3: Atmospheric Pressure

The Earth is protected by the atmosphere. The atmosphere is a layer of gas that covers the Earth to a height of about 700km.

The gases of the atmosphere exert atmospheric pressure. On the surface of Earth, this atmospheric pressure is about 100,000Pa.

If you have an open can, there are equal forces in all directions, so the shape does not change. If the air is removed from the can, it collapses.

As you move away from the surface of the Earth, atmospheric pressure decreases as there are fewer particles of air pushing down.

P1.3.4: Liquid Pressure

Water exerts a liquid pressure. Water molecules are close together. They will collide with each other, the container and anything in the water. Liquid pressure acts in **all directions**.

Pressure increases with depth as there are more particles pushing down. You can demonstrate this with a bottle of water with holes punched at different heights. The lower the hole, the further the water travels due to the higher pressure as more water molecules are above pushing down.

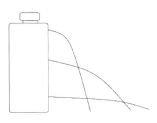

The denser the liquid, the greater the pressure exerted at the same depth. This is due to there being a greater weight of liquid pushing down in the denser liquid.

You need to be able to use the formula for calculating pressure in a column of liquid:

Pressure (Pa) = Height of column (m) × Density of liquid (kg/m³) × Gravitational Field Strength (N/kg)

This is given to you on the Physics Formula Sheet.

Don't forget that if you are asked to calculate the total pressure then you need to add the liquid pressure and atmospheric pressure together.

P1.3.5: Floating and Sinking

Items float when the upthrust balances the weight.

For an object that floats on the surface of water, the water exerts a larger upwards force on you than the downwards force exerted by the air.

Pressure (Pa) = Force (N) ÷ Area (m²)

An object will float if:
(Pressure at bottom x Area at bottom) – (Pressure at top x Area at top) = Weight

Submarines are able to float at different depths. Their structure has tanks which are either filled with air or water to adjust the depth it floats at.

To make the submarine sink, you fill the tanks with water which increases the weight.

To make the submarine surface, you fill the tanks with air which decreases the weight.

Check Your Understanding

1. Explain why gases exert pressure.

2. In which direction does the force exerted by a gas act in?

3. What is the relationship between pressure and volume?

4. Explain why atmospheric pressure is lower on the top of a mountain than at sea level.

5. Explain why placing holes at different heights in a bottle of water leads to different horizontal distances being achieved by the jets.

6. Explain how submarines can float at different depths.

P2 Forces

P2.1.1: Speed

To calculate speed, we need to measure:

- Distance – With a ruler
- Time – With a stop watch or light gates

The light gate is a more accurate method of recording the time as it eliminates the human reaction time that impacts on stop watch use.

Ultrasound can also be used to measure distance. The device measures the time taken for a pulse to travel to an object and back.   It then calculates the distance using speed and time.

Speed (m/s) = Distance (m) ÷ Time (s)

In uniform motion, the speed doesn't change. In non-uniform motion the speed changes.

Useful conversions:

1 km = 1000m

1 mile = 1609m

1 hour = 3600s

Remember to always check the units you are using.

P2.1.2: Vectors and Scalars

Vector: A quantity that has a direction and a magnitude (size).

Examples:
- Forces are represented with an arrow where the length shows magnitude and the direction shows direction.
- Displacement: Distance from a point in a particular direction. Can be written as 2 miles east or +2 miles.
- Velocity: How fast something travels in a given direction.

Scalar: A quantity that has a magnitude (size) but no direction.

Examples:
- Time
- Distance: How far you have travelled.
- Speed: How fast an object travels.

You can assign positive values to a certain direction. The opposite direction is negative.

This is vital when you come to add vector quantities. E.g. when you are calculating relative velocity.

If car 1 is travelling east at 40mph and car 2 is travelling west at 60mph, we can say car 1 has a velocity of +40mph and car 2 has a velocity of -60mph.

The relative velocity of the two cars is +40 - -60 = 100mph (as the two minuses become a plus).

P2.1.3: Acceleration

Acceleration: Change in velocity per second.

> **Acceleration (m/s²) =**
>
> **Change in Velocity (m/s) ÷ Time (s)**

When calculating acceleration, we need to consider if it is positive or negative. If the car is increasing in velocity, it is positive acceleration. If the car is decreasing in velocity, it is negative acceleration.

Use the right sign: + or -

The acceleration due to gravity is 9.81m/s^2 or about 10m/s^2. Use this for any falling objects.

P2.1.4: Distance-Time Graphs

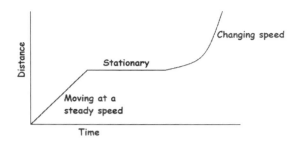

Horizontal line: Stationary
Diagonal line: Object moving at a steady
speed.
Curved line: Object moving at a changing
speed
Gradient of the line: Speed

To find the gradient of the line:
1.   Draw a right-angled triangle under the
line.
2.   Find the change in distance and the
change in time.
3.   Substitute into the speed formula.

Distance-time graphs show the total distance travelled.

Displacement-time graphs can have a positive, zero or negative gradient. The gradient is the velocity.

To calculate velocity from a displacement time graph:

1. Draw a right-angled triangle under the line.
2. Find the change in displacement and the change in time.
3. Substitute into the velocity formula:
Velocity = Change in displacement ÷ Change in time

Exam hint: Look carefully at the y axis label to know what kind of graph you have.

P2.1.5: Velocity-Time Graphs

When looking at velocity-time or speed-time graphs, the gradient of the line tells you the acceleration. For a speed-time graph this is just a magnitude. For the velocity-time graph, this is magnitude and direction.

> *Exam hint: Look carefully at the y axis label to know what kind of graph you have.*

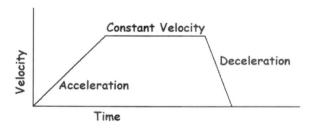

Horizontal line: Constant velocity
Diagonal line: Constant acceleration.
Curved line: Changing acceleration
Gradient of the line: Acceleration

To calculate the acceleration:
- Find the change in velocity and the change in time.
- Substitute into acceleration formula:
Acceleration =
Change in Velocity ÷ Change in Time

Distance is the area under a speed-time graph.
Displacement is the area under a velocity time graph.

Exam hint: If asked to calculate areas under a graph – Split the area up into shapes you know the formula to calculate area of. E.g. rectangles and triangles

P2.1.6: Equations of Motion and Kinetic Energy

You need to be able to apply the equation given on the Physics Formula Sheet:
(Final Velocity)^2 – (Initial Velocity)^2 = 2 x Acceleration x Distance

Example:
When dropped, a book falls a distance of 1.5m with an acceleration of 9.8m/s^2. Calculate the final velocity.

Stage 1: Write down what you know
Initial Velocity = 0m/s
Acceleration = 9.8m/s^2
Distance = 1.5m

Stage 2: Rearrange the formula to make final velocity the subject.
Final Velocity = $\sqrt{}$((2 x Acceleration x Distance) + (Initial Velocity)^2)

Stage 3: Substitute in and solve.

Final Velocity = $\sqrt{((2 \times 9.8 \times 1.5) + (0)^2)}$

$= \sqrt{(29.4 + 0)}$

$= \sqrt{29.4}$

$= 5.42217668469$ m/s

$= 5.4$ m/s (to 2sf)

<u>Kinetic Energy</u>

The units of energy are joules. They have the symbol J.

Energy store: System where you can do a calculation to find the energy associated with it.

> **Kinetic Energy (J) =**
> **0.5 x mass (kg) x (speed (m/s))²**

Check Your Understanding

1. What is the formula to calculate speed?

2. Explain the difference between a scalar and a vector.

3. What is the formula to calculate acceleration?

4. Explain how to draw a distance-time graph for a cat that walks 5m at a steady speed in 60s then stops for 30s.

5. Explain how to calculate speed from a distance-time graph.

6. What does the gradient represent on a velocity-time graph?

7. What is the formula for calculating kinetic energy?

P2.2.1: Forces and Interactions

Newton's Third Law:
"For every action there is an equal and opposite reaction."

Pairs of forces arise when objects interact. In an interaction pair:
• Each force acts on a different object
• The forces are the same size and type
• The forces act in opposite directions

Non-Contact Forces: A force produced because an object is in a field; the objects do not need to be in contact for the force to act.

Field: Region where an electrical charge; magnetic material or mass experiences a force.
E.g. Electrostatics; magnetism and gravity
Forces are vectors.

Forces are represented on diagrams by a force arrow. Force arrows for non-contact forces are usually drawn from the centre of the object.

Contact force: A force that only acts when objects are in contact. Contact force arrows are drawn from the point of contact.

Examples of contact forces:
Friction; drag; normal contact force and upthrust

With friction the interaction pair would be:
The force of the ball on the surface and the force of the surface on the ball.

P2.2.2: Free Body Diagrams

Free body diagrams show the forces acting on a single object. They are usually drawn with a dot or box and the force arrows to show the forces acting on it.

Steps to drawing free body diagrams:
1. Identify all the non-contact pairs.
2. Identify all the contact pairs.
3. Focus on a single object. Draw that object with arrows showing all the forces acting on the object.

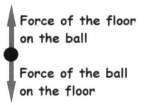

Force of the floor on the ball

Force of the ball on the floor

Resultant Force (net force): The force when two or more forces are added together as vectors.

Sometimes forces act at different angles to each other. You can use Pythagoras' theorem to calculate the resultant force of two forces acting at 90° to each other.

E.g. Calculate the resultant force of a 2.0N force and a 5.0N force acting at 90° to each other.

Step 1: Draw a diagram showing the forces.

Step 2: Use Pythagoras' theorem to work out the hypotenuse.

$$c^2 = a^2 + b^2$$
$$= 2^2 + 5^2$$
$$= 29 \ N^2$$
$$c = \sqrt{29}$$
$$= 5.4N$$

You can work out which two forces at right angles add up to a particular force by resolving the force in two directions.

If you draw the force and angle on graph paper you can use a ruler to work out the components.

E.g. Resolve a force of 50N acting at an angle of 40 degrees into two components.

1. Select a suitable scale e.g. Use 1cm = 10N
2. Mark start point on the graph paper.
3. Measure 40 degrees and mark.
4. Draw 5cm line at 40 degrees.
5. Draw the other two lines to make a right-angled triangle.
6. Measure the lines. This gives the forces.

P2.2.3: Newton's First Law

Newton's first law of motion:
An object will continue to stay at rest or move with uniform velocity unless a force acts on it.

To change the speed or direction (motion) of an object, a resultant force is required.

If the resultant force is zero, then the speed or direction of the object does not change. Moving objects keep moving; stationary objects do not move.

Inertia: The measure of how difficult it is to change an object's velocity.

If the speed or direction of an object does not change, the resultant force is zero. So, a steady speed has a resultant force of zero.

Equilibrium: An object is in equilibrium if all the forces cancel out – The resultant force is zero.

P2.2.4: Newton's Second Law

If the resultant force is not zero, it can:
- Change the speed
- Change the direction of motion
- Change both speed and direction.

If the speed or direction of an object changes, it is accelerating.

If we consider a tennis ball being dropped, the force of the Earth on the tennis ball is greater than the force of the air on the tennis ball. This means it will accelerate towards the ground.

Newton's Second Law states that the acceleration the resultant force produces on an object depends on:
- Size of the resultant force
- Mass (inertia) of the object

Force (N) = Mass (kg) x Acceleration (m/s²)

When considering experiments with force, mass and acceleration we should keep the following in mind:

- The ramp must be compensated for friction (raise the ramp until the trolley moves down at a steady speed)
- Use light gates to record time (removes problems with reaction time and human error)

An object that moves in a circle at a constant speed is accelerating as it is constantly changing direction. To enable an object to travel in a circle, a force directed towards the centre of the circle acts on the object. E.g. satellites in orbit

P2.2.5: Everyday Forces

Terminal Velocity

If we consider a skydiver, as they jump out of the plane, the force exerted on them by the Earth is greater than the force the air exerts on them, so they accelerate.

As they accelerate, the force of the air increases. Eventually the force of the air equals the force of the Earth of them. They fall at a steady speed. This is terminal velocity.

When the parachute is opened, the force of the air increases which reduces velocity. Eventually the lower terminal velocity is reached as the forces balance.

Objects that move horizontally also reach terminal velocity.

54

Forces at Angles

If you are dealing with forces acting at different angles, you need to resolve the forces so you only deal with forces acting in two directions at right angles.

To do this you need to draw a scale diagram using the angles given. You can then measure the line representing the opposing force and convert to N by using your scale.

Rockets

Burning fuel pushes gases out of the bottom of the rocket. The gas pushes on the rocket and the rocket pushes on the gas. When the force of the gas on the rocket is greater than the force of the Earth on the rocket, it lifts off.

P2.2.6: Momentum

Momentum is a vector that depends upon:
- Mass
- Velocity

> **Momentum (kg m/s) =**
> **mass (kg) x velocity (m/s)**

In any collision, momentum is conserved.
(Law of conservation of momentum)
This means the momentum before has to
equal the momentum after.

Elastic Collisions

This is a collision in which kinetic energy is
conserved. In an elastic collision, the
energy in the kinetic store stays the same.
A moving object colliding with a stationary
one would stop moving and the object it
collided with would move off at the exact
same velocity.

Inelastic Collisions

This is a collision in which kinetic energy is NOT conserved. Some energy is transferred to other stores such as to a thermal store by sound. They are collisions where the end velocity of the combined objects is lower than the original objects.

P2.2.7: Work and Power

Work: The transfer of energy.
Uses forces to transfer energy between
stores. Usually work is done against
friction or gravity.

Work done (J) = Force (N) x Distance (m)

E.g. Miranda is shopping. She travels up an
escalator. Calculate the work done when
Miranda travels from the bottom to the
top of the escalator.

9.7m

7.8m

510N

Work Done = Force x Distance
= 510N x 7.8m
= 3,978J

*Exam hint: Remember use vertical distance
on questions using stairs or escalators*

Power: Rate of transfer of energy.

Power (W) = Work Done (J) ÷ Time (s)

E.g. You run upstairs in 1.2 seconds. Your weight is 500N and the vertical height of the stairs is 3m. Calculate the power.

Power = Work Done ÷ Time
Work Done = Force x Distance

Work Done = 500N x 3m
= 1500J

Power = 1500J ÷ 1.2s
= 1300W

Exam hint: If you can't calculate the final answer using one equation – Think about what you can calculate to get you there

Check Your Understanding

1. Explain Newton's Third Law.

2. Give an example of a contact force and a non-contact force.

3. Draw a free body diagram for a book on the desk.

4. Explain Newton's First Law.

5. Explain Newton's Second Law.

6. Explain the motion of a base jumper.

7. What is the momentum formula?

8. What is the work done formula?

9. What is the formula for calculating power?

P2.3.1: Stretching Springs and PAG P2

You need two or more forces to compress, stretch or bend an object.

Materials can be either plastic or elastic:
Plastic: Material does not return to its original shape when the force is removed.

Elastic: Material will return to its original shape when the force is removed.

Investigating Springs

1.   Attach a spring to a clamp on a clamp stand.
2.   Measure the spring's initial length.
3.   Place a 1N weight on the spring.
4.   Measure the new length and record the extension.
5.   Repeat for more weights.
6.   Repeat each weight 3 times and calculate the mean.

Safety to consider:
- Clamp the clamp stand to the desk to avoid it tipping over.
- Keep feet clear of the working area.

Accuracy considerations:
- Get to eye level for measuring lengths
- Ensure the spring isn't bouncing when you measure

A graph of force against extension of a spring is a straight line up to a certain point called the limit of proportionality. The force and spring have a linear relationship until the limit of proportionality. This is Hooke's Law.

The spring has an elastic limit. Below the elastic limit, the spring returns to its original length when the force is removed. Beyond the elastic limit, the spring is permanently deformed.

Force exerted by a spring (N) =
Spring Constant (N/m) x Extension (m)

To calculate the spring constant from the graph, you need to work out the gradient of the linear section.

The spring constant tells you how stiff a spring is.

P2.3.2: Stretching Materials and Storing Energy

If you are asked to calculate the energy transferred when a spring is stretched, you need to be able to use the formula from the Physics Formula Sheet:

Energy transferred in stretching (J) = 0.5 x Spring Constant (N/m) x (Extension (m))^2

Exam hint: Go careful with units. If they give you lengths in cm then convert to m.

Remember that energy transferred is also work done.

Not all materials obey Hooke's Law. Elastic has a non-linear relationship between force and extensions.

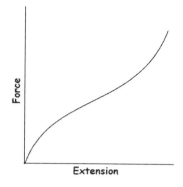

The graph shows the non-linear relationship between force and extension for an elastic band.

When materials deform, they store energy. Scientists design materials that either transfer energy back when they regain their shape (tennis rackets) or are permanently deformed on impact. E.g. crash barriers.

P2.3.3: Gravitational Fields and Potential Energy

Gravitational field: Region where a mass experiences an attractive force.

Gravitational field strength or gravity constant, g: Measure of the force on a 1kg mass when it is in a gravitational field due to another mass.

The mass does not change but the force on the mass depends on the field.

The force acting on an object in a gravitational field is larger if:
- Mass is larger
- Distance between them is smaller

Gravity Force (N) = Mass (kg) x gravitational field strength (N/kg)

Exam hint: g on Earth is 10N/kg

Weight: The force due to gravity that acts on an object.

> **Weight (N) = Mass (kg) x Gravitational Field Strength (N/kg)**

> *Exam hint: Don't confuse mass and weight. Mass is measured in kg. Weight is a force so measured in N.*

g can also stand for the acceleration due to gravity.

> **Resultant Force (N) = Mass (kg) x acceleration due to gravity (m/s^2)**

Acceleration due to gravity on Earth is 9.81m/s^2.

When you lift an object in a gravitational field, you transfer energy to a gravity store. This energy is called gravitational potential energy.

GPE depends upon the mass and height of the object.

GPE (J) = Mass (kg) x Height (m) x Gravitational Field Strength (N/kg)

P2.3.4: Turning Forces

Pivot: The point about which forces act to produce turning effects.

Moment: The turning effect of a force. Moments can be clockwise or anticlockwise.

The moment depends upon the size of the force and the distance from the pivot to the point the force acts.

The closer the force is acting to the pivot, the harder it is to produce a turning force.

> **Moment of a Force (Nm) = Force (N) x Distance (m)**

The direction of the force and the distance measured are at 90 degrees to each other.

E.g. Calculate the moment when a 4N force acts downwards at a distance of 3m from the pivot.

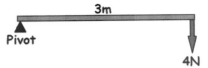

Moment = Force x Distance
= 4N x 3m
= 12N m clockwise

An object is balanced if the anticlockwise moments are equal to the clockwise moments about the pivot. This is the principle of moments.

It can be written as:
Force x distance on one side of a pivot = Force x distance on the other side of the pivot.

P2.3.5: Simple Machines

Lever: A rod, or other object that won't bend, with a pivot. A force applied at one end produces a force in the opposite direction at the other end. It can be used to transmit a rotational force.

Force multiplier: A factor that greatly increases the effectiveness of a force. A lever is a force multiplier.

The effort is the force that you exert on the lever.

The load is the force you are trying to move.

Mechanical Advantage: The ratio of load to effort.
Mechanical advantage = Load ÷ Effort

The work done by you is equal to the work done on the load.

E.g. Calculate the mechanical advantage of using a wheelbarrow to lift the load.

Calculate the force:
Effort = (Load x Distance from pivot to load) ÷ Distance from pivot to effort
= (400 x 0.3) ÷ 1.2 = 100N

Calculate the ratio of the load to effort:
400N ÷ 100N = 4

Gears behave like a lever that rotates.

The ratio of the diameters of the cogs tells you the ratio of the effort and the load.

A bigger cog will exert a greater force but will not move as far. Force x Distance in each case is the same.

Gears can be used to change the direction of the rotating force or the speed at which it rotates.

Other force multipliers include:
- Pulleys
- Ramps

P2.3.6: Hydraulics

Fluid pressure produces a force that acts at right angles to any surface.

The force that is exerted by the fluid depends upon:
- Pressure
- Area

Pressure (Pa) = Force (N) ÷ Area (m^2)

The greater the pressure, the greater the force.

Increasing the area of the surface will increase the force.

A hydraulic machine is one that uses a fluid to transmit a force.

E.g. Hydraulic lifts or car jacks. These allow us to use a small force to lift heavy objects.

Hydraulic brakes stop cars when we use a small force on the brake pedal.

Hydraulic machines work because it is almost impossible to compress liquids.

Check Your Understanding

1. Explain Hooke's Law.

2. Describe an experiment to find the spring constant of a spring.

3. What type of relationship do elastic bands demonstrate?

4. What is the formula to calculate gravity force?

5. Explain the difference between mass and weight.

6. What formula is used to calculate gravitational potential energy?

7. Explain why it is easier to open a door when you push far from the hinge.

P3
Electricity

P3.1.1: Electrostatics

Protons have a positive charge.
Electrons have a negative charge.

Subatomic Particle	Relative Mass	Relative Charge
Proton	1	+1
Neutron	1	0
Electron	0.0005	-1

Atoms are neutral overall as they have the same number of protons and electrons.

When you rub two insulators together, electrons can be transferred from one to the other. One object ends up with extra electrons making it negatively charged. The other object has more protons than electrons making it positively charged.

Remember: Only electrons move

When an acetate rod is rubbed with a cloth, electrons are transferred from the rod to the cloth. The rod has more protons than electrons so becomes positively charged. The cloth has more electrons than protons so becomes negatively charged.

When a polythene rod is rubbed with a cloth, electrons are transferred from the cloth to the rod. The cloth has more protons than electrons so becomes positively charged. The rod has more electrons than protons so becomes negatively charged.

Opposite Charges Attract
Like Charges Repel

When an object is connected to a piece of metal, the charges can flow and the object becomes discharged.

Sparks can also discharge objects. A spark is a flow of current through the air.

There is an electric field around a charged object or particle. Placing another charged object in this field means it will be attracted or repelled.

If another charged object is placed in the electric field, the field lines will stretch. The force on an object will be in the same direction that causes the field lines to shorten and straighten. The closer together the field lines, the stronger the field is. The direction of the field lines is the direction of the force on a positive charge.

P3.1.2: Electric Current

Current: Rate of flow of charged particles (electrons).

To make current flow, you need a cell, battery or power supply and the circuit must be complete.

The current anywhere in a single closed loop is the same.

Conventional current: Current flows from the positive terminal to the negative terminal. It is in the opposite direction of electron flow.

Charge Flow (C) = Current (A) x Time (s)

Charge is measured in coulombs (C).
Current is measured in amperes/amps (A).
Time is measured in seconds (s).

P3.2.1: Circuits and Potential Difference

Component	Symbol
Cell	—┤├—
Battery	—┤╎╎├— / —┤├--┤├—
Power Supply	—∘ ∘—
Switch	—◞ ◞—
Lamp	—⊗—
Ammeter	—Ⓐ—
Voltmeter	—Ⓥ—
Fixed Resistor	—▭—
Variable Resistor	—⊘—
LDR (Light dependent resistor)	—▭—
Thermistor	—⊘—
Diode	—▷⊢—
LED (Light emitting diode)	—▷⊢—

You need to know the circuit symbols from
the table above.

Potential difference (p.d.) is required for current to flow in a circuit. It is caused by the separation of charges inside a cell/battery. This makes one side positively charged and the other negatively charged.

The positive terminal has a higher electrical potential than the negative terminal.

Potential difference is measured in volts (V) with a voltmeter.

The positive terminal on a cell has the longer line.

The negative terminal on a cell has the shorter line.

When a p.d. is applied between the ends of a wire, an electric field is set up inside the wire.

Electrical working: Method of transferring energy from chemical stores to chemical components.

> **Energy Transferred (J) = Potential Difference (V) x Charge (C)**

Example:

A defibrillator has a potential difference of 500V and needs to transfer 250J of energy.   Calculate the charge.

Charge = Energy Transferred ÷ p.d.
= 250J ÷ 500V
= 0.5C

P3.2.2: Series and Parallel Circuits and PAG P7

Series Circuits

In a series circuit, the current is the same everywhere.

Current is measured using an ammeter. An ammeter is placed in series.

Voltmeters measure the potential difference across a component. They are connected in parallel to the component.

The drop in potential across a wire is very low so the voltmeter would read zero if placed across a wire only.

A voltmeter measures the rise in potential across a battery/cell. It measures the drop in potential across a component.

The readings on all voltmeters across the components will equal the reading across the battery.

$$V_s = V_1 + V_2$$

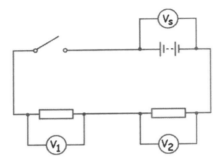

Parallel Circuits

The current in all the loops, add up to the current near the battery.

$$A_1 = A_4 = A_2 + A_3$$

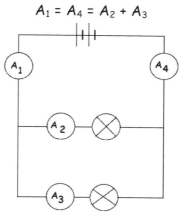

The potential difference across each component is the same as the battery.

When building circuits, there are times that it does not work. To identify the source of the problem:

- Connect the bulb to the battery, if it doesn't work, try another battery.
- If that doesn't work, try changing the bulb.
- When they work, check each bulb.
- Replace one lead to check the other leads you wish to use work.

Connect the ammeter so the negative terminal is nearest the negative terminal of the battery or the reading will be negative.

P3.2.3: Resistance

Current depends upon the potential difference and resistance in a circuit.

Resistance is measured in ohms (Ω).

Current is a dependent variable. It can only be changed by changing the p.d. or resistance.

p.d. (V) = Current (A) x Resistance (Ω)

Ohm's Law: Current is proportional to the potential difference if the temperature does not change.

A metal is made up of positive ions arranged in a regular pattern. Electrons have left the outer shell of the metal atoms to form the positive metal ion and the electrons are delocalised.

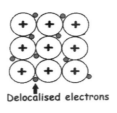

Delocalised electrons

The delocalised electrons are free to move. Resistance is produced when the electrons collide with the metal ions.

A thinner wire will have greater resistance than a thicker wire as there is a greater chance of the electrons colliding with the positive metal ions. The same is true of a longer wire.

Variable resistors can be used to change the amount of wire the current flows through and so changes the resistance. E.g. dimmer switch.

P3.2.4: Graphs of p.d. and Current

A characteristic graph is one that has current against potential difference.

It requires measurements of current flowing through a component at different potential differences to provide the values to be plotted on the graph.

Remember to reverse the connection on the battery/power supply and repeat the measurements to provide negative values.

These measurements can be used to:
- Calculate resistance
- Plot a characteristic graph (p.d. on x axis and current on y axis)

Linear circuit element: Component that has a resistance that does not change.
E.g. Resistance wire or fixed resistor

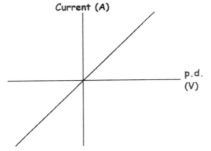

Non-Linear circuit element: Component that has a resistance that <u>does</u> change.
E.g. Lamp

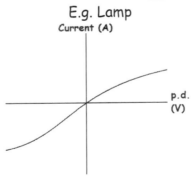

As the electrons collide with the metal ions in the wire, the ions vibrate more. This makes the wire get hotter and causes more collisions. Notice how the gradient on the line changes showing the resistance is not constant.

Diodes only let current flow one way. Some emit light = LED (Light emitting diode).

As p.d. is applied in the forward direction, very little current flows then rapidly increases. Reversing the p.d. means no current flows.

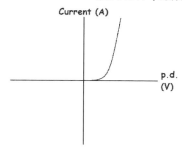

P3.2.5: LDRs and Thermistors

Thermistors

The resistance of a thermistor changes with temperature. It is made of a semiconducting material (silicon). The electrons present in the atoms of a semiconductor do not need much energy to escape to form the current.

As the thermistor is heated, electrons gain enough energy to escape from the atoms in the semiconductor so resistance drops.

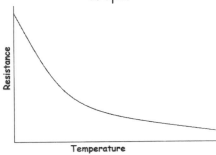

LDR

A light-dependent resistor (LDR) has a different resistance with light intensity. It is made of a semiconductor. Light causes electrons to be released to increase the current.

As the light intensity increases, more electrons are released in the semiconductor and resistance decreases.

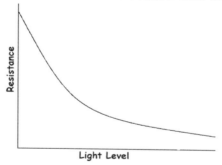

P3.2.6: Net Resistance and Circuit Calculations

Net resistance: The resistance of a circuit if all the components were replaced with a single resistor.

The net resistance will change if the components or their arrangement is changed.

If an identical lamp is added in series:
- The current decreases
- The net resistance increases

If an identical lamp is added in parallel:
- The total current increases
- The net resistance decreases

Series Circuits

We know in a series circuit:
- Current is the same everywhere
- The p.d.s across each component add up to the p.d. across the battery.
- $V = IR$

Example: Find the resistance of the variable resistor.

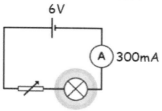

Stage 1: Write down all you know.
Battery p.d. = 6V
Current = 300mA or 0.3A
Resistance of lamp = 15Ω

Stage 2: Work out the p.d. across the lamp

$$V = IR$$
$$V = 0.3 \div 15$$
$$V = 0.02V$$

Stage 3: Work out the p.d. across the variable resistor.

$$V_{VR} = V_{cell} - V_{lamp}$$
$$= 6 - 0.02$$
$$= 5.98V$$

Stage 4: Work out the resistance of the variable resistor.

$$R = V \div I$$
$$= 5.98 \div 0.3$$
$$= 19.93\Omega$$

Parallel Circuits

We know in a parallel circuit:
- The p.d. is the same across each loop
- The current in each loop adds up to the current near the battery.
- $V = IR$

Example: Find the resistance of the lamp.

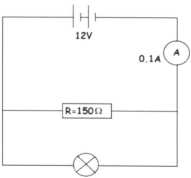

Stage 1: Write down what you know.
Battery p.d. = 12V
Current on ammeter = 0.1A
Resistance of resistor = 150Ω

Stage 2: Work out the current through the resistor.

$$I = V \div R$$
$$= 12 \div 150$$
$$= 0.08A$$

Stage 3: Work out the current through the lamp.

$$I_{lamp} = I_{battery} - I_{resistor}$$
$$= 0.1A - 0.08A$$
$$= 0.02A$$

Stage 4: Work out the resistance of the lamp.

$$R = V \div I$$
$$= 12 \div 0.02$$
$$= 600\Omega$$

P3.2.7: Sensing Circuits

Thermistors can be used to control heating or air conditioning units. The p.d. changes with the varying temperature and so circuits can be built to switch on temperature control systems by using a thermistor.

A LDR can be used to monitor the light levels in a greenhouse and turn on lights as needed.

A variable resistor can be used to monitor door positions as the resistance changes with how much it turns.

A pressure sensor can be used in a burglar alarm as it senses pressure.

P3.2.8: Electrical Power

Power: Rate of transfer of energy.
Units: Watts (W)
May also have kilowatts (kW) or
megawatts (MW).
1kW = 1000W
1MW = 1,000,000W

Power (W) = Potential Difference (V) x Current (A)

**Energy Transferred (J, kWh) =
Power (W) x Time (s)**

Power (W) = Current^2 (A) x Resistance (Ω)

You may choose an appliance that has a
higher power rating as this will carry out
the task in a shorter time.

Check Your Understanding

1. Explain what happens when you rub an acetate rod with a cloth.

2. What is the formula to calculate charge flow?

3. Explain what is meant by the term current.

4. What is the formula to calculate energy transferred when given p.d. and charge?

5. What can be said about current in a series circuit?

6. What can be said about the p.d. in a parallel circuit?

7. How do you calculate power?

P4 Magnetism and Magnetic Fields

P4.1.1: Magnets and Magnetic Fields

If two bar magnets are placed together:
- Like poles repel
- Opposite poles attract

Field lines represent magnetic flux. The number of field lines passing through a particular area is called magnetic flux density or magnetic field strength.

When two magnets interact, they will move in the direction that makes the field lines shorten.

There are two types of magnet:
1. Permanent magnet: Magnetic even when other magnets or current is removed.

2. Induced magnet: Magnet produced when a magnetic material is placed in a magnetic field which may or may not stay magnetic when it is removed.

The domain model of magnetism says a permanent magnet is made up of many small magnetic regions (domains) that all line up.

Iron or steel have regions that are not lined up. When placed in a magnetic field, they do line up. This makes them an induced magnet.

In some magnetic materials, the domains remain lined up once the magnet is removed. In others, the domains return to their original direction.

Compasses point towards the magnetic north pole. The Earth behaves as if there is a large bar magnet at its centre. Scientists think the Earth's magnetic field is caused by convection currents in the molten iron core of the Earth.

P4.1.2: Currents and Fields

When current flows through a wire, there is a magnetic field around it. A single wire has a series of concentric circles as the shape of the magnetic field. If the current is flowing towards you, the field lines are anticlockwise. Reversing the current, reverses the direction of the magnetic field.

Exam hint: Use your right hand to work out the direction of the field lines. Thumb points in direction of current – fingers curling shows the direction of the field lines.

To show a wire produces a magnetic field when current flows through it:
- Connect a wire into a circuit of cell and switch.
- Place a compass under the wire.
- When the current flows, the compass will align with the field produced.

The magnetic flux strength (or magnetic flux density) depends on:
- Magnitude of the current (bigger = stronger)
- Distance from the wire (closer = stronger)

The strength of a magnetic field is measured in teslas (T).

A solenoid is a coil of wire. Having lots of loops makes a stronger field. To increase the strength of the field further, a magnetic material can be placed in the centre of the coil. Placing a magnetic material in the core creates an induced magnet when the current flows.

Electromagnets can be made which are much stronger than any permanent magnet.

P4.2.1: Currents and Forces

If a current-carrying wire is placed inside another magnetic field, the two magnetic fields interact. The two magnetic fields push on each other and create a force on the wire. The force on the wire is always at right angles to the magnetic field.

When two fields that are in the same direction are put together, they add up.

If two fields that are in opposite directions are put together, they cancel out.

A catapult field has fewer stretched lines below. The wire will move down so all field lines straighten. This movement shortens the field lines.

Fleming's left-hand rule
Most important point: Use your LEFT hand!

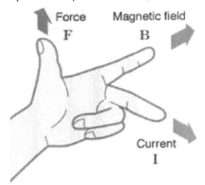

The direction of the force tells you the direction of movement.

The size of the force depends upon:
- Current
- Length
- Magnetic flux density / strength of the field

P4.2.2: Motors

If a loop of wire is placed in a magnetic field, the force generated on each side of the loop when the current flows will make it turn.

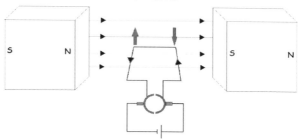

To make the coil spin continuously, the current needs to move in on the right and out on the left. This is achieved with the use of a split-ring commutator.

The split-ring commutator allows the current to flow the same way from the battery but change halves of the coil as it spins.

The force on the left side of the coil is always up and the force on the right side is always down.

The speed of the motor can be changed by changing:
- The magnitude of the current
- The strength of the magnetic field
- The number of coils in the wire
- The length of the coil

P4.2.3: Electromagnetic Induction

If you move a wire in a magnetic field so that it cuts field lines, an induced potential difference is produced across the wire.

This can also be achieved by making a magnetic field change around a conductor.

If the wire does not cut the field lines, no induced p.d. is produced.

You can increase the induced potential difference by cutting more field lines per second by:
- Moving the wire faster
- Using a stronger magnetic field
- Using more wire (more coils)

If you connect the wire to a circuit, a current will flow. When current flows in a conductor, a magnetic field is produced. If the wire is in a magnetic field, a force acts on it. The magnetic field produced is in the opposite direction to the field that produces the p.d.

If you drop a magnet in a metal pipe, the magnet induces a current in the pipe. This current produced a magnetic field. The direction of the current opposed the change in the magnet's field repelling the magnet and making it fall slower.

P4.2.4: Generators

Alternators

In an alternator, the coil of wire spins between the poles of a magnet. This generates an alternating potential difference as the potential difference changes direction. This generates an alternating current (a.c.).

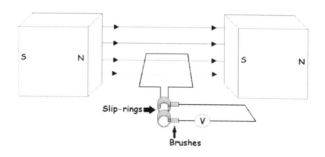

The brushes are not attached to the slip rings. They brush against them so the circuit is always connected but the coil does not tangle.

Dynamo

A dynamo generates a direct current (d.c.). This means the potential difference that drives the current does not change direction. This is achieved by using a split-ring commutator.

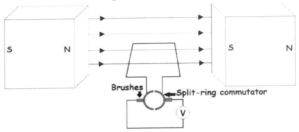

The direction of the p.d. does not change as the coil is connected to a split-ring commutator, however, the magnitude of the p.d. does change.

The output of both alternators and dynamos can be increased by:
- Using a stronger magnetic field
- Using more turns on the coil
- Spinning the coil faster

P4.2.5: Transformers

Transformers increase or decrease the potential difference. The p.d. is induced when the magnetic field lines cutting a coil change.

You can change the field lines cutting a coil in 3 ways:
- Move the magnet or coil
- Use another coil and turn the current in it on/off
- Use another coil with an alternating current

When current flows it produces a magnetic field. If the coil is turned on and off, you change the number of field lines cutting the second coil. If an a.c. is used, the field lines constantly change as the current changes direction.

A transformer is a loop of iron with two coils. The magnetic field is *trapped* inside the iron core.

An alternating p.d. across the primary (1°)coil produces an alternating current in the primary coil. This produces a magnetic field in the iron core that is always changing. This induces a changing p.d. in the secondary (2°) coil.

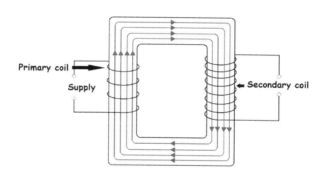

You need to be able to use the formula from the Physics Formula Sheet:

P.d. across 1° coil ÷ P.d. across 2° coil = Number of turns in 1° coil ÷ Number of turns in 2° coil

Example:
Your phone charger changes the mains p.d. of 230V to 12V. If there are 400 turns in the primary coil, calculate the turns in the secondary coil.

Stage 1: Write down what you know.

Exam hint: Use a simple diagram to help you get the information in the right place.

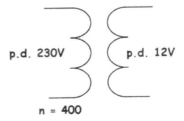

p.d. 230V   p.d. 12V

n = 400

Stage 2: Rearrange the formula to make the number of turns in 2° coil the subject.

Number of turns in 2° coil =
(P.d. across 2° coil ÷ P.d. across 1° coil) x Number of turns in 1° coil

Stage 3: Substitute in and solve.

Number of turns in 2° coil =
(12 ÷ 230) x 400
= 21 turns

Exam hint: Remember that the number of turns must always be a whole number

Step-up transformers increase the p.d. by having more turns on the secondary coil compared to the primary.

Step-down transformers decrease the p.d. by having more turns on the primary coil compared to the secondary.

P4.2.6: Microphones and Loudspeakers

Microphones

Dynamic microphones are like generators. A sound wave is a pressure wave. As the sound wave hits the diaphragm of a microphone, compressions (areas of high pressure) push the diaphragm in and rarefactions (areas of low pressure) pull it out.

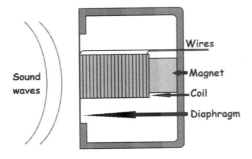

As the diaphragm moves in and out, the coil does too. This induces a potential difference across the ends of the wire. This the electrical signal.

In a carbon microphone, there are carbon granules behind the diaphragm.
As the sound wave hits the diaphragm, it changes the resistance of the carbon.
A current passing through the carbon granules will change as the resistance changes.

<u>Loudspeakers</u>

A loudspeaker is like a motor.

A varying alternating current is produced by an amplifier. The current produces a force on a coil of wire as it is in a magnetic field. This makes the cone move in and out and produces a sound wave.

The movement of the coil depends on the size of the p.d.

Check Your Understanding

1. Explain the difference between permanent magnets and induced magnets.

2. What does the strength of a magnetic field depend on?

3. Explain how to work out the direction a wire moves when in a magnetic field.

4. Explain how a motor works.

5. Explain why a magnet falls slowly through a metal pipe.

6. Explain how an alternator works.

7. Describe the difference between step-up and step-down transformers.

8. Explain how dynamic microphones work.

About Wright Science

Wright Science is a YouTube channel created by Vicki Wright, a secondary science teacher in England.

I started Wright Science as a resource for my own classes to have extra help outside of school time. It started with a single recap video for each exam back in 2013 and then just grew. These days there are videos for every lesson on both the separate science courses and combined science courses which are used by a number of students across the country and world!

I hope that you find this book useful and welcome your comments.

Good luck in your exams!

Printed in Great Britain
by Amazon